CW01630737

] ye

The Jesmond Year in Haiku

Keith Jewitt

LAUREL BOOKS

What is this life if, full of care,
There is no time to stand and stare?

W. H. Davies

In a Magpie's Eye

The Jesmond Year in Haiku

To my brothers
Rob and Alan

First published in 2017 by Laurel Books
282 The Common, Holt, Wiltshire BA14 6QJ

Printed by Quorum Print Services Ltd
Units 3&4, Lansdown Industrial Estate,
Gloucester Rd, Cheltenham GL51 8PL

Poems © Keith Jewitt 2017

The rights of Keith Jewitt to be identified
as the author of this work have been asserted
in accordance with the
Copyright, Design and Patents Act 1988.

British Library Cataloguing in Publication Data
A CIP record for this book is available
from the British Library

ISBN 978-1-873390-16-0

January to March

FOREHAIKU

Write down what you see
in seventeen syllables,
no more and no less.

Five in the first line,
seven in the second and
five more in the third.

NEW YEAR'S DAY

Calibrating fourth
dimension, small explosions'
smoke hides pigeons' flight.

Magpie's clatter-clack –
the one note rhythm-song of
Winter's discontent.

Gale's toss in wall's lee –
undergrad bin-bags, tin-cans,
fine sacrificed twigs.

Hornbeam leaf, last of
last year's cling-ons: waving and
drowning in wet wind.

Leaf-free trees give us
long sight: monochrome squirrel
twitching as it runs.

Limping crow zig-zags
bin to bin: put to flight by
insistent traffic.

King Cushat* flaps knaves
off scaffold: blackbirds scuttle
rat-like under cars.

*Cushat – wood pigeon

Fine-feathered, cocky,
mallard by his pond: waiting
like the grim sower.

Rained-on streetlamp top –
slimy turtle's back throwing
off herring-gulls' feet.

"Zi Zou Zuh Zuh!" says
the tit: so tits in the know
will know what is his.

Magpies in leaf-mess
like miniature badgers, scratch
and sniff the right stuff.

Cushat on cushat
ridge tile MMA: loser,
at gable end, flies.

Silver trunklets, bronze
leaflets: beech hedge pretending
it's still in Autumn.

The long-tailed tit's fuss
in the hornbeam's mouldy moss
rewards my long stare.

Exotic blossoms,
on limbs too slim for cherries,
are the first to show.

Crickety singing
of an invisible bird
in a leafless tree.

Along the North Wall
the underworld's crocus bulbs
shower gold upwards.

Under his tail, the
squirrel's still: not lunch break but
a break in his lunch.

Stepped-on puppy noise
of herring gull contesting
dormer perch with crow.

Rhododendron buds
fat hard green: prepurtenant,
eager as bullets.

Damp orchard labels
pledge inconceivable fruits
from acne of buds.

Flying to black sites
repetitive rendition –
magpies with big sticks.

High, sceptical, the
year's first kestrels both soar and
hover on still air.

Fat frog in a box
alive, spawn-stuffed: sexton's gift
to the allotments.

The vasty laurel's
waxy winter canopy
puts the Spring in shade.

Return to dullness –
fat cushats shredding blossom
for no clear reason.

Singing scaffolders
unwind shackles clenching tight
equinox blossom.

Hornbeam buds, pustules
of upward snot or eye-gunge –
but they are budding.

Student lunch fall-out
feeds fearless jackdaws, lurking
on library lawn.

Force-fields of strong song,
site and species-specific,
dam out the Winter.

Magpies knit their nest –
over, under, sideways, down
in ivied holly.

April to June

Avocado shape,
raspberry ripple colour –
dropped magnolia.

Seeing they're seen by
fat pink egg-eater, magpies
turn their nest away.

Cherry-tree crow's song –
three caws, and on the third
a blossom of steam.

Under the feeder
King Cushat sees off magpies
stealing scattered seeds.

On the broom's top, King
Cushat is enthroned: like Plante
Genet* in reverse.

Facing the West wind,
soprano magpie bleats till
parent finds and feeds.

Abhorring vacuum,
King Cushat treats unnumbered
car park space as his.

*Henry II wore a sprig of broom, Plante Genet in French, in his hat and so became known as 'Plantagenet', which in turn gave his dynasty its name.

Jackdaws in mown grass
swish and swagger: crops empty
but styling it out.

Rice on the road draws
two crows. Car-rage defeats them,
dignity intact.

Gothic pinnacles
or catkins: laurel blossom
arrived with the bats.

Upward baby-hands,
downward poodle-ears: hornbeam
and horse-chestnut leaves.

Staccato holmgang*
in near-darkness: two cushats
up a barren ash.

Acrobat cushat
gnaws twig-tip beech shoots: folded
wings for safety net.

Eternity now –
this blossom, this day, with a
poet's jug and loaf.

*Holmgang was a form of Norse judicial duel. The two contestants stood on a small island (a holm) and the first to be driven off or killed was deemed to have lost the suit.

Pulled pear: the blackbird
gleans from the overflowing
shopping bag of life.

Jackdaw hogs pavement
yumming up protein-rich chunks
of fresh spruce-green phlegm.

Two crows, one squirrel
advance and riposte till all
leave the piste unhit.

Squirrel-scalped large limbs
are budless: lime's tiny twigs
emit ginger spikes.

Stick-wielding cushat
kendos into ivy to
fortify the nest.

Clock clack, cricket's back:
calling the year's stages in
lands too cold for chirp.

Porsche's fussing boom
drives car park squirrel back to
rest in his laurel.

Out with the bluebells –
rhododendrons in palest
Barbara Cartland pink.

She's stuck in the nest,
he's out magpieing alone –
two have become one.

Eslington House pink
shockinger than puce: blossom
of a tree in heat.

Blackbird so busy
in bus stop leaf-drift, I can
see his dirty face.

Hunched grey-caped shoulders
ruched by North wind: sparrowhawk
zooms off draughty perch.

Jehovah's Witness
taking no for an answer
and earning a smile.

First leaves on the lime –
a cushat squats the old nest,
stands, preens and moves on.

Fight or flirt? Blue tits'
willow pattern airprox, by
hornbeam's velvet leaf.

Spring's pink fall: blossom
loose in Osborne Road distracts
Lollipop Lady.

Pink mist by the drain –
blossom's afterness going
to its underness.

Pink blossom puddles,
shining puddles of rain, wait
for sun and blow-dry.

Spotted woodpecker's
indecisive bouncing flight –
neither up nor down.

Laburnum nodding
to buttercups on the lawn –
it was all yellow.

Dwarf bijou pygmy
green cherries rattle on red
rhododendron bleed.

Pasties clamped to mouths
students ambling: following
crow nabs pastry flakes.

Car park mayblossom
spreads honey on the air and
ice cream on the bush.

Sycamore's first flight –
conjoined green flops, little V
signs to the heavens.

Damped down flies gobbled
by first swifts, petite martins –
sun breaks clouds, damp flies.

Hyper-violet
steroid blue: raging bloom of
a ceanothus.

Mayblossom's fall – its
stingless honey reduced to
spotty confetti.

Blackbirds bickering
sound fury: moon shadow bats
kill then back to black.

Back into the bush –
the last scabs of mayblossom
retreat like herpes.

Top note of champagne
or whiffy old tom cat: it's
elderflower time.

Three grim North summers
Rosamond Lehmann saw this
privet bush flower.

July to September

Ontological
question: what's it cushats eat
in July holly?

Puddle and hawthorn
wash and card sparrows' feathers
outside Weight Watchers.

Due diligence of
young magpie on used tissue
and ASDA receipt.

Fresh pink guts bubble
out of road-flat rat: and the
bubbling flies go in.

"IN" and "OUT" care home
gateposts: they're not opposites,
merely shades of shade.

Kestrel flying school –
Dad Wingco, Mam (Air Traffic)
Kees them in to base.

Ash to ash across
the mansion lawn: kestrels learn
to fly in short hops.

Urgently fledging
kestrels' airshow scares gulls, though
the calls are not threats.

However much I
watch the kestrels, they see me
more than I see them.

The silence of the
kestrels tells me they're coming
of age: but am I?

Two magpies tweet, voice
unbroken: beggars not thieves,
parents retreating.

One-legged wagtail
hop-swoops to pluck a seed from
a squashed tomato.

No hoo-hoo answers
her kee-wick: she's alone, or
mistress of the wood.

Jackdaw youth, hoodless,
struts urban blades, confident
in his gatherings.

Summer's fall – lime twigs
with bast* shock-cord, drying to
kindle Winter's fire.

*Bast is the fibrous layer between the bark and the inner wood of the lime tree: when a lime twig breaks, the bast holds the twig together in the same way as shock-cord connects tent poles.

Swifts have fledged and gone
the swallows fidget on wires
sun dims, apples glow.

On the lawn, filing
my feet: feeding sole's fragments
to unseen eaters.

Leaping poodle snaps
jaws shut on orbiting wasp –
then chews daintily.

Autumn trumps first fart –
leaves of conkerless chestnut
dangle rhubarb-red.

Caterpillar green
elderberries on stalks
like mauve capillaries.

Cushat's greasy end –
dashed against the high windows
of the poet's flat.

Wrap on the railings,
red ribbon in the gutter,
Osborne Road Monday.

Clayton House TO LET –
sycamore flight path clear, car
park conkers unsquashed.

Conker on concrete
plop: noise of sappy green leached
out of spotted leaf.

Sycamore prop-blade's
flat-spin seed-drill fights 1*g*
right down to the ground.

Rage in dying light –
she-owl, he-owl, owlets gone
time enough to fight.

Flaming carotene
in leaves all Summer: now no
chlorophyll masks it.

October to December

Pavement conkers and
ash-keys: passively fighting
to be next in life.

Close up wren appears
paradoxically small
also unafraid.

Cobnut's pavement click
pods out seeds on barren ground
where only words sprout.

Tit-shit squitters sparge
leaf squidge spongle-white. Flown nests'
blown felts float on air.

Lime leaf lollipops,
dead yellow/living green: points
of lemon and lime.

Frantic squirrels run
trembling branch tip to branch tip
from cold, thief of life.

Leaf-fed, hornbeam limbs
live: pale, quilled, show over, leaves
won't see in New Year.

Ash: bunched key-dottels,
leaf comb-over. Sycamore:
verdant, with black spot.

Hard red apples fall
untempting: gravity sticks
one to a pruned stub.

Rain on the plane tree –
Midas tears on gold slip slide
to granite gravel.

Over head-high hedge,
late allotment sunflowers
reach for sunless sky.

A stormless Autumn's
colours: beech chargrilled lemon,
cherry pink as fruit.

Bunched, fistic: hornbeam's
brown leavings shade the magpies'
Autumn strategy.

Rain-battered split pea
yellow lime leaves' fall unhides
laurel's green triumph.

Grey prey: tree'd squirrel
derides uplooking cat with
downward gutturals.

HALLOWE'EN

Witches' hats, apples'
insufficient buoyancy,
turnips' inner light.

BONFIRE NIGHT

Bird emergency –
red parcel airdrop feeds them
berries' stone and squish.

Holly's red, as if
on 60's colour telly,
floats free of its green.

Leafless lime borrows
evergreen ivy's scarf – but
debts must be repaid.

Inside bare hornbeam
magpie circumvolates and
pecks at empty twigs.

Parent-toddler gang
scoops wild apples over wall
with pink fishing net.

Windswept ridge-tile crow
fluffs up his downy black heart
needing winter coat.

The world's shrunk with cold –
flying like flies, tits buzz bare
trees on tiny quests.

Squirrel ravelling
bast from lime's split ends: then back
to his laurel home.

Leaf-blower blare spooks
squirrel: stotting leap startles
statuesque cushat.

Holly berries tempt
cushat from perch: tail over
bill, losing his cool.

Alpine traverse takes
blackbird within nibbling range
of treetip berries.

Cushats grown agile
stripping the holly now wait
for December's crop.

Gale-blown squirrel scrags
crouching cushat: resulting
violence calms him.

Juvenile gull grips
pizza slice, flees downwind from
adult piracy.

Unfancied by birds,
Metro tunnel tree shows its
berries to the sun.

Perched cushat unmoved –
free to do nothing, as if
only time could fly.

Eight o'clock tawny
owl or hooting boy's tipsy
imitation game.

Downwind of the ash –
hopeful keys in pavement sog
and halcyon sun.

NEW YEAR'S EVE

Seventeen magpies –
as many songs as there are
days left in the year.

AFTERHAIKU

Knowledge is power:
vision trumps all the senses:
only poets stare.

Reflect and forget –
the gone-by year is buried
in a magpie's eye.